Flow —— Winged Crocodile

A Pair / Actions Are Erased / Appear

Flow — Winged Crocodile

A Pair / Actions Are Erased / Appear

Leslie Scalapino

chax
tucson
2010

ISBN 978 0925904 93 5

Cover photos © 2010 by Steven Schreiber, and taken by him at
The Flea in December 2009.

Published by   Chax Press
                    411 N 7th Ave Ste 103
                    Tucson, Arizona 85705-8388
                    USA

Printed in Canada by Friesens

CONTENTS

for Michael McClure and Amy Evans McClure

Flow—Winged Crocodile is a play in two acts separated by a pause in darkness. The tone of the play is light comedy for a charge of combustion by the performers who are sprightly seeming to push on any balance accruing there (where they are in it) until it spills over (as if the performers are in reference to an imaginary line) vomiting outside by it being inside (as if inside and outside is in them, and in us, the viewers). Directions may say that an actor "says gorgeous puking." This is to be done by their enacting their words as if words are 'the gorgeous outside.' As such the actors are elegant, never shouting or gross.

FLOW — WINGED CROCODILE

ACT I

The three performers who speak are young women, the play demonstrating simultaneous conflict and serene balance between the left and the right side of a person's brain: LEFT-SIDE OF THE BRAIN and RIGHT-SIDE OF THE BRAIN are questioned by and in conversation with TANYA.

    LEFT-SIDE OF THE BRAIN (L) is a young woman wearing a black slinky dress. RIGHT-SIDE OF THE BRAIN is a young woman wearing a colorful dress of purple, red, green. TANYA is a young woman dressed to imitate the appearance of Patty Hearst in the photos of her in the bank heist with the SLA: she wears jeans, a beret, maybe a partial Patty-Hearst mask, and carries a toy AK47.

    A fourth performer, who never speaks, is a dancer, the CROCODILE-MICHELIN-RHINO, dressed in a sheer puffy grey suit like the Michelin man (not bulky thick, the suit allows the movement of her body to be seen); she has small green wings on her back as the winged crocodile, and a small grey horn on her forehead like a rhino. As rhino she charges, crumples, charges, somersaulting. Yet her dance is subtle, humorous, frenzied (that could be when slow). CROCODILE-MICHELIN-RHINO is apparently chaos and violence but in the course of her dance during the play she transforms that description: revealing that she is the body, pure kinetic daemonic motion that has no language—but a manifestation equal to and alongside the left and right sides of the brain. She's a daemon, a highly skilled clown. I wrote the part for the dancer Molissa Fenley. The dancer dances to music by Joan Jeanrenaud, Strange Toys, tracks 2, 6, 7, and 10.

Where there are paired poems, the left side is read vertically first, then the right side read vertically. These are displayed in this manner to demonstrate on the page the left and right sides of the brain at once. Throughout the play the performers speak line breaks only as casual conversational phrasing never stilted. Although they recognize rhyme in their passages, that emphasis is as spoofing their own thoughts and actions as they're doing actions and speaking these. Sometimes they sound as if they are speaking inner shape, casual conversation, and reading doctrine given to them—all of these at once. When one speaks a phrase in quotation marks, she is quoting someone else and herself at the same time. The sound, as the syntax of the poems, is an interior/inner that's only heard (by the performers and by the audience) intuitively.

The set is a bedroom, completely ordinary except the furniture is very tall in relation to the people: a high bed on the audience's right side of stage (with a sign above stage that reads "RIGHT SIDE") and a tall tea table at the audience's left side of stage (with a sign above the stage reading "LEFT SIDE"). There are three very small children's chairs. The performers use these chairs both to sit in (they may sit in the small chairs at the tea table—which is too high for them to reach its top—as they're drinking from imaginary tea cups) and from which to climb onto the bed and onto the tea table. The performers never look at the dancer (green-winged CROCODILE- MICHELIN-RHINO with one horn); they do not ever see her while she charges and crumples amongst them. Nor is the audience seeing the performers' imaginations either, as they speak of the hologram of winged CROCODILE-MICHELIN-RHINO: They don't create her as their imaginings, she is in a separate, simultaneous realm.

TANYA stands (audience's) center-left; LEFT-SIDE (L) stands stage left by tea table; RIGHT-SIDE (R) stands stage-right near the bed.

Winged CROCODILE-MICHELIN-RHINO runs in from the side and does a wild dance to music track 2, slowly, lightly charges (soft somersaulting), then crumples to knees, then charges. She ends her soft charging and crumpling before the others begin to speak. CROCODILE-MICHELIN-RHINO sits on floor, still. Music and dance end.

TANYA comes forward to center edge of stage. She stretches one arm as if it's just morning, the other arm cradling an AK47. She speaks to the audience, gesturing to either side of her to indicate L and R:

TANYA   the two parts
of the brain
equal at once
       race
together always
       seemed
in conflict
or (oar) serene

Green-winged CROCODILE-MICHELIN-RHINO at LEFT-SIDE'S first words begins, without music, minimal movement suggesting she will charge, crumble; she does one somersault. L, R, and TANYA throughout the play do not ever look at the dancer.

L stands in front of tea table, looks at audience while speaking this as fast rushing gorgeous puke:

L   A hologram of MP
        shows her to be
        a winged crocodile
        dismembering people
        whirring into them as
        swimming in them in a
        different light also a
        charging rhino that kneeling
        gets up and butts others
        in a crowd with her horn.

R stands in front of bed, looks at audience while speaking this as fast rushing gorgeous puke:

R   As
        the winged crocodile
        that
        swims in blood
        the hologram shows
        her hating women x-
        cluding them from work
        or recognition which she
        determines to herself
        and her few pets men.

TANYA moves to small child's chair and sits throughout CROCODILE-MICHELIN-RHINO'S minimal movement without music. TANYA, not noticing the latter, is hurling-immersing herself:

TANYA   She screams
                at the women
                massed like
                        birds

"You (wade) *walk*
　　behind the men
　　　　the men,"
　she screams "are
　who enjoy
　　　　(mine) this"
L (looks up, irrelevantly)
　Employed
　from
　being
　a pet
　high
　expire
　fill
　place
　of others.

　　　　There's no action

TANYA begins sipping from imaginary tea cup. CROCODILE-
MICHELIN-RHINO dances to music track #6, comes up to an
imaginary line in front as if it is barring her, and dances there, then is
drawn backwards and forward charging again. Dance and music end.

L still standing in front of tea table gazing at R as consumed in seeing:

L　　Everything
　　is consumed
　　a few plates are laid out
　　and she gobbles at every one
　　　　in the room.

R still in front of bed gazing at L as consumed in seeing:

R   on the floor
             her pets
             and she leading them
             are given everything
             a dog and pony
                     show.

TANYA passionately to R and L:

        TANYA   "one
                     is seamless
                       whole
                     winged crocodile
                     (hologram) thinks
                     but mechanical games
                     see by not being *one*"
                     MP thinks
                     "but one person created
                     is inside and outside
                       two/too"
                     outside person
                       thinks.

Winged CROCODILE-MICHELIN-RHINO charging runs off stage.

R using small chair gets up and stands on the bed speaks to L rushing flow:

          R   The pets are deified
                   future—she says
                   (theirs) future "tradition"

                    as such emptied games
                              as hierarchy in it
                    self—present being *one's*
                    self is incorrect dis
                    Elision fields dained—games
(this is said sententiously)   "empty as self is (always)."

R on bed and L by tea table speak to each other as if the two sides of the brain alter each other now:

L   Each exists
         on a plain empty as all
         linked to each other
                    produce
                    alter
         flow continually.

R   When, on medicine,
         O.D.ed, an accident,
         the characteristic
         of the brain
                    became
                    clear
         that it is
                    recurrence
         to recycle
         and recycle in one
                    (person).

L using small chair gets up on tea table, runs around on it as if she's trying to find a comfortable spot on the table the way a dog digs in its

bed to soften a spot, she finds such a spot with her feet and stands
there, nonchalantly speaking her subject unrelated to running on the
table:

L   For her, though—games
        are (empty)
        tradition of that game
               as such
        is hierarchy/higher
        than anyone changing
        it—they're excluded
          and nothing

CROCODILE-MICHELIN-RHINO rushes in, somersaulting. Stands
doing minimal motions without music.

L standing on tea table vomiting the invisible outside:

L   Except for herself
        "women"—she says
        can't change their
        hierarchy and "only"
        —may be anything—
        by speaking/doing *men's*
        these ideas in their mode"
            fixing a single way

R standing on bed vomiting the invisible outside:

R   While
        the nation (is) to be
        may be led by the waiting in the wings
        Barbie doll with horns

                              she's
              who says they're of/the people, while
                    have always said/
              are saying give the rich/huge
              tax breaks wildly not of the
                                        people

---

*L casually reorients herself to find a different comfortable spot on tea
table:*

L   So—where were we—?
         seeing

*TANYA seated in child's chair at tea table gets up from chair and
cranes her neck:*

TANYA the two parts
       of the brain
       equal at once
                   race
       see opposite alter
       a
       (the same) thing they
                          see.

R tests spots on the bed as if she is getting her sea-legs:

R   The   man
         de   mand
         ing racism—his
         asserting his
                    view

by/and in meeting in
public saying *my*
      observing
his being being that—
      is *'I'm*
immature *Rebel*
Without a Cause.'

TANYA   Say that happened—!?
            —as if 'So what" or
            —"I don't believe you"

CROCODILE-MICHELIN-RHINO runs off stage.

        TANYA gets up on the bed goes to the head of it,
        further end from audience, other end from R.

*L ignores R and speaks as if the behavior of the man she's describing
is an event that happened to herself, reversing him in the terms of his
own senses—so she's saying utter freedom:*

L   My seeming to him thwarting his
        authority (my just discovering this) as
        he's scorning that *there is present-being-free*
        —*at all*—my sense there *is* (that)—*by*
        there being no authority *then*
            (in 'present' *or* in 'being')

*TANYA ignores both L and R; she is either explaining the same man's
behavior or appropriating the event as her own. She's standing at the
head of the bed, further from the audience than R who is at the end
of the bed—TANYA picks up a pillow and says the rushing motion:*

TANYA He scorns that
present-is-*being-only-no*-authority-*then*
when there's no authority
even by every thin being at once
there
—and connecting—in—and producing
the gorge/ space, movement

firmament-movement

TANYA steps down from bed

L steps down from table, speaks passionately unified (as the continual
double, the pair, of opposites):

L The man
de mand
s authority
there being it
has contempt for
there's
(no)
present-being-free
(is)
by no-authority *then*

R standing on bed on shaky sea-legs speaks happy
as if carried on a flood:

R While
the nation (is) to be
may be led by the waiting in the wings

                              Barbie doll with horns
                                        she's
They all look   who says they're of/the people, while
off into the audience   have always said/
                                        are saying give the rich/huge
                                        tax breaks wildly not of the
                                                                people.

*R, L, and TANYA stop looking at audience. Then CROCODILE-
MICHELIN-RHINO comes in from behind them: as if charging,
crumples charges throughout their exchange:*

L   Actions have
         structure
         apparent
                 ly
         not as a *whole* later?

*TANYA gets up on tea table, runs around on it feeling with her
feet for a soft spot, as a dog paws its bed; she settles on a spot
and standing on it says as if they're gorgeous unified labor:*

                    TANYA While games are nothing 'inner'
                                   because set rules?
                           the nation (is) to be led
                           by the Barbie doll with horns
                           who says she's/they're
                           the people, while saying
                                   they've always said
                           "give the rich huge tax breaks"
                           and they'll want to put some in/
                           back—bilk everyone for the people

open fools

what is the Barbie doll with horns

thinking?

*CROCODILE-MICHELIN-RHINO stands amidst scene doing minimal
movement without music. L, standing beside tea table looks up at
Tanya, says gorgeous puking:*

L   A winged crocodile .

     guts—in their face

     the foreigners—in their country

        who'd

     been—now dead—occupied

     wade in sewage—not fixed yet

     (not repaired by Haliburton)

     —while the woman also rhino

         in hologram

     kneels charges crumples charges

*CROCODILE-MICHELIN-RHINO stands still amidst them.
R, L, and TANYA are matching each other, cheerfully grandly modestly
vying, as if on a line of speaking and attention, they call to each other
while standing separate from one another:*

R   saying the men her pets big

     names have to be added, she

     cancels others/society is obliterated

         in cronyism

     everything has to have big names

L, standing next to tea table, realizes:

L I think we should obliterate

   society—and then—it will begin

TANYA, standing on tea table, comments dryly:

TANYA   I don't believe that any more

L bursts racing:

L   Barbie doll with horns
        has no senses   touch and
        taste buds?
        s rule of law the men
        cronies put in office
        however incompetent skim
        off
        the whole are power

R, standing on bed, lifts off racing:

R   A hologram of
        the winged crocodile
        who swims
        eating the legs of the
        foreigners we've caught
        and fleeced for oil bombs
                go off in hotel
        frequented by whole govt

R and L speak to each other the sensation of having burst, equal,
racing:

L   the two
        coincide at
                ban

books the Barbie
doll with horns
tries to—and to
fire the librarian for
not banning them—and
MP bans the books
if not written by men pets
list of books that's hierarchy.

R   what is 'inner'
is 'outside' making
'inside' outside of outside
not itself when inside
    outside inside
that's the *inside outside*
is the most troublesome,
the present.

*Winged CROCODILE-MICHELIN-RHINO RHINO dances to music
track 7. Dance and music end. She sits on floor at back center of
stage wagging/swaying her head to herself:*

L, standing beside tea table, gorgeous puking, to R:

L   I needed to change the way
I *used* to see—I was using
a line—as if horizon—to see
any event hold to the line in space
    or separate on it
    separating from it?
Submitting all events
    to this line
    to float

to see them
ultimately
this didn't work—or rest in space.

TANYA, *standing on tea table, gorgeous puking, to audience:*

TANYA MP comes to the line
                   she
    (sings softly)
    who only transgresses space
    Barbie doll with horns and
    hologram of MP as winged crocodile
                and as rhino at once
    butts the crowd with her horn, charges
    ahead of Barbie doll with horns
    in the outside (in society).

CROCODILE-MICHELIN-RHINO, *who has been limply light sack seated on floor, does one soft lumpy beautiful somersault in TANYA'S speech.*

L *sits down in one of the small children's chairs next to tea table; she's swallowing bitter bile:*

L   Asking the man
      —in the black robes—
      for advice, he said
      "The trouble with you is
      you mix seeing
      with your *being*/seeing
      so, *be* seeing then—is what is
      —*you* do that
      Whereas *I* don't," he says. "I separate these."

R, standing on bed, searches for words —addressing L—she mimes oaring:

R   To view every appearance—/all appearances—
before, these/coming to outside-horizon line/or/
swimming on it (oar)—
in (as *his*) tradition-authority—(I can't say this)—
(it's hard to articulate this)—:
there's no seeing being *then—ever.*

L, still sitting in child's chair, says with pure innocence addressing R:

L   They wouldn't get started

He has his tradition-authority—pre
formed thought of his—as the *end*
/beginning for anyone—*only.*

*TANYA, still standing on tea table, in sincere innocence utters to audience
the center of the dilemma:*

TANYA   while—in *his*—
no present ever
or being,
there'd be *description*
outside—of it/one outside
being described:
rather than one ever being.

That's why
I'm
in terror
the two parts
when
seeing— other

L still seated in small chair — to R:

L   pick up the
          back structure
          he thinks (imposes)
          present being is
          tradition *too* (outside's
                    not free). As such,
          we're being only tradition
                    which
          he sees as only authority

R begins to happily jump on bed — to L:

R   this is
          back structure
          because it's bothering me
                    as *mine*
          it isn't behind, driving
                    the *war*

                    is it?

               TANYA, standing on tea table, answers R:

          TANYA   Yes everything —
                         here

Tanya pauses then utters, quizzically:

Tanya   I don't know why

          people smoke

when it hurts them

*R gets down from bed, stands on child's chair, speaks as if she doesn't
know the word "genitals":*

R   lying Dionysus
            sprawled basking
            his chest and geni
            tals spread out on him

TANYA swoons standing:

TANYA   Supposing he's
                gentle
                too? having
                by senses invented
                love too—has?

*CROCODILE-MICHELIN-RHINO rolls and thrashes on the floor, starts
before L speaks.*

---

*L seated beside R, both in children's chairs utter to everyone the
outside as gorgeous puke:*

L   The dog and pony show
            is brought to town
            —everywhere—in each/town—
            and each time
            is presented—by her as the only
            thing there is—if the new's

a product—why should they
care?

R So the Barbie doll with horns
keeps jabbing the opposing can
didate with how *his* former religious
leader is a fanatic while in *her*
religion everyone thrashes seized by the
god and asserting our boys go to
push out demons
his war for him their having spoken to
him.

L asks the air, vaguely:

L Dionysus?

TANYA answers L sternly:

TANYA No!
Keep up.

CROCODILE-MICHELIN-RHINO is still.

L stands up beside tea table and speaks in simple passion to audience:

L O.D.ed with
medicine
a painkiller,
an accident,
I was trapped in endless recurrence.

*CROCODILE-MICHELIN-RHINO, beginning at "seeing," comes
forwarding one rush somersaulting flipping effortlessly. Then throughout
L's speech, she does very minimal movement without music:*

                    seeing
            the brain recycles
                    whatever trash
            is put into it.
            It has nothing either in it
            self or outside

            the brain can only make
            through this trash outside events
            one is in endless actions
                    of them in it

        L continues:

                            suffering terribly in
                            —there being only—
                            hallucinations—in endless
                            pain physical-mind passages
                            —I was in the campaigns

            sometimes the brain's recycling
            is broken through
            in this state
            of recurrence my brain
            sometimes
            broke through to dreams—in me

                            the brain
                            breaks through to

a dream *not* of suffering:

in one

dream: I

step out on top red tiered vast outside
buttes, mesas, huge red gorge with a crack
in the center pouring water-flow off
the billion stairs of the red crack forge through
which the water-flowing down billion-stairs
                              gorge   plateau
innumerable horses are running
toward me. I walked in it toward the crack
from which the horses pour
by without touching me. "They won't hurt me
/won't trample me" is a thought said

> *R has climbed up on bed; standing on bed,*
> *sarcastic toward L and her vision:*

          R   flow
                   ing
                   cracked
                   that's
                   a
                   croc
                   a
                   dial

TANYA standing on tea table, in bliss, gives the victory sign at the
word "two":

TANYA   the whole
         state
         de (di)
         regulated
         goes
         —state of bliss
             —two

                    R standing on bed, comments dryly:

                    R   There's a flaw
                            in this—
                            other—
                            endless—
                            numbers of actions
                            —*do*
                            enter.

TANYA and R in bliss:

TANYA   The   con
                  can
         di
         date
         condition of lies
         always
         day
         separated by night

                    R   All
                            the
                            time
                            enters

TANYA sardonic spoofs the world's confusion, pushes the
words out on a line in the air:

TANYA   in one
                               news
                               paper the stories
                               have *no*
                               organization—first
                               it's the mafia
                               has the country—then
                               health
emphatic   *here*

L ignores TANYA, speaks   The crowd weeping
ecstatically to audience: with joy—entranced
                                there is change

END OF ACT I

THE TRAINS

ACT II

The Trains is ACT 2 of *Flow—Winged Crocodile*. ACT 2 follows after a pause in darkness. The set and costumes are the same as in ACT 1 except that CROCODILE-MICHELIN-RHINO over her sheer grey puffy Michelin suit with one grey horn on her forehead and green wings, twice also appears in a black robe, the second time discarding it while dancing.

When one says words or phrases in quotations, she is imitating both someone else and herself. They produce balance pushing this to spill over vomiting invisible outside.

PAUSE IN DARKNESS. THEN LIGHTS

CROCODILE-MICHELIN-RHINO waits in the wings unseen.
TANYA is standing on the bed looking like Patty Hearst. With one
hand she holds a toy AK47, and with the other hand she appears to
pull down an imaginary pull-string, that would be used to stop a train.
TANYA appears to speak to herself in victorious shout:

TANYA   WuWuWuWuWuWuWuWuWuWuWuWuWuWuWu
GoStop!

L in front of tea table looks over and notices TANYA. Observing TANYA,
L speaks to herself:

>> Apparently she's both
>> stopping it and
>> urging it on with her
>> cries.

L speaks to audience with pure joy:

L   The Vote
new—the leader
counsels us—we
could/can have *hope*

for
having/we have
driven the corrupt
lying govt greed
y fueled by war causing
it—

out—the crowd weeps
with joy

*R stands in front of the bed on the audience's right side of stage. She
doesn't notice TANYA but responds to L's speech The Vote, speaking
with pure innocent joy:*

    R   The crowd weeping
                with joy—entranced
                    there is change

L continues to speak to audience:

L   The characteristic
       of the brain
         became
          clear
       recurrence
        to recycle
         and
      recycle in one,
          person.

                R speaking blissfully to herself:

    R   No, I thought

            the two parts

of the brain
equal at once
race
together always
seemed
in conflict
or (oar) serene

*R climbs up on bed in front of TANYA (who is on the bed) and jumps
on it, her actions happy, her words puking the gorgeous bile:*

R   Recycle on the part of the man in
black robes   she's
seeming to him thwarting his
authority as
he's scorning that *there is present being*
free

scorns that
there are
ones who *are* being free
—at all/*is the* present free
at all/*is* the present
—but (on the contrary) that's *seen*
in reality

R explains her words/the previous passage:
present is seen, and as seen
and as present—*is* free

—that's what that *is*—
    all at once

L happily begins to hop hopscotch on invisible lines on floor:

     L   My friend
then—(she was hit by a van)—
         something happened
                       from
         space as seeing
             base in infinite
        —people—low venal

R walking around on bed:

     R   The fault is—old hardline—
         with having stories, that
              everything
         is stories form
         everything—*Don't have*
                 any!
         don't own

TANYA has been standing on the bed all this time holding her AK47,
says serenely entranced:

     TANYA   can't be free
                    we're spectacle
                       limit them
                    outsides of people
                    spectator spectacle

L gets up on small child's chair, climbs up on tea table, speaks as if
swept forward on falls-rapids:

L   —suddenly—
                    —she was hit by a van—and
                    —unharmed miraculously—she sees—
                    spectacle as there outside spectator sees in
                    infinite space?   *the*
                    (one) no longer spectator part of and in
                                                space—*there*

          will be no change

                                        there
                    we've base motives—venal low
                                        there?

in the country—the *new*
          president
          from the new
will be no change—she says
negatively reverses *there*
          everything—
unharmed miraculously—
she was hit by a van—*then*
          reverses the space

L's tone alters from ecstasy; tempered, she explains:

                    No, I mean,
                    while we're the crowd
                    when we're weeping with joy
                    there's already no chance

—the woman says—hit by a van
later (now) can say, *See*
the space unfolding the same
outside *is*

TANYA on bed opens her arms in the air, sardonic:

TANYA   *if* there are—the
                marvels
        it's one's brain
        seeing—the outside of the
                        outside?

R is helpful, happily exlaining:
R   line of pre-judgment
their   judging—all are
         negative—there could be no
there   without hope there's no action
         future—then that's found to be
         comforting by the negative inverse
                    one
         no moving away, or as future is
         not there except as this view.

There, not as open
is future as or moving by
comforting one—by not being or forgiving.

L standing on tea table:

L   hell bliss black
           ness the ascending and
           diving glittering flying winged
           at once descending and ascending
           not horizon in that no space
           at the same black red blood flowers
           not being able to forgive one
                              self or them/some

TANYA is still standing on the bed, sardonic to L and R:

TANYA   Opposite is
                denied
                a toilet—
                they gripe,
                seize on it
                (the issue), to gripe,
                entitled,
                though they're
                not entitled to it,
                heightens them

                    the dense
                      light
                    winged box

L minimally jumping hopscotch on tea table to TANYA:

L   The crowd
        weeps for joy as

no one had this
view hope
of one as them ever before
they're a crowd having
joy by virtue
of that *(being a crowd)* at once

R standing on child's chair to L and TANYA:

R   regardless
of any future actions
—is it

TANYA the brain recycling breaks through to
dream outside of only outside?

L still standing on tea table in inexpressible pain as marvels, her speaking staggered floating as if triggered by TANYA's words—speaks to herself as if to everywhere:

L   Dream breaking through hallucinogen that was
accidentally induced in me:

the horses   pour

ing
on the crack that's where the billion-tiered
stairs/sides of the red mesa meet they're galloping
from the opening onto the crack midst the
vast ranges of other red mesa-gorges everywhere the
outside red billion-stairs in the middle of these I

walk on the crack all stairs meeting there I walk toward
the opening where the innumerable
horses come out galloping the stream of them in
passing me don't trample or touch me
'they won't hurt me' is thought.

L quietly:

L   the brain
        recycles—only—is
              from
        something happening
              the *outside*
                    it
        is nothing in itself?

R gets off bed and sits down in small child's chair by bed—to L:

R   Another friend, of many years—no,
         she's *not* "friend—ha!"—says "You
         only bullied me—because you're a bully
                I accepted
                you [BLANK] speaking to me"
sardonic   (beginning twenty-five years ago)

R continues, addresses herself:

The customs
of our/their commun
ity don't actually mirror
the law—ever—which she knew

/knows—yet then uses the law
to get everything away
from one as/in that—community
       from it

               the dense
                 light
              winged box
               to kill

L standing on tea table looks over at R sympathetically:

L   Hit by a van—a different person—and
                    from it—?
                unharmed miraculously—this one sees
                    everything
              negatively reverses *there*
                 will be no change

             —anything
                  spectator part of and in
                     the—the—
            infinite space—*from*
                     it?

*R, oblivious of L, goes on talking to herself; second passage begins with
its title:*

R   Why didn't you say something *then?*

(when you're being bullied into being a friend?)

> The Court Conceiving
> not valuing—work of the humble—*has*
> removed them from outside—that is—*reversing*
> the *public space*

L gets down from table using small child's chair, then as if changing
her mind or getting a fresh start she gets up again on the tea table:

L   the humble—all are—ruled
                      by the court to have rights
                                  of livelihood—*in*
                      public space—yet seeing them
                      on the sidewalks, the only *place*
                      their humble work
                      has the court ruled they're
                                  infringing public space
                      there
                      disrupting others' space charged
                      they're banned, they're removed
                                                  from it?

TANYA gets down from bed. R moves to small chair by tea table,
looks up at L, explains:

R   the court first ruled all
                                              have
                      the humble have rights of
                      work—in public space—outside—seeing
                      the humble on sidewalks to be
                      infringing public space the court bans them.

TANYA is jumping hopscotch on invisible lines near tea table:

TANYA Why is the court thinking
      that—*reversing*
  the public space
  as others' space/*being*—seeing's *infringing*
  —infringed by the humble
  working—outside—is not value d?

     L could be talking about "the friend" or talking
     about TANYA—L gestures vaguely yet in the midst
     of wonders:

     L   She negatively reverses
        all stupid and low only corpse
           float s   ing
        in iridescent limb

L—as a new idea—logic and wonder:

       If
    we're
    stupid low
      no
    hierarchy
      exists!

R gleefully gets up on small chair and stands on tea table, flaps her arms:

    R   birds
      plant—flower—with no words

                    plant—flower—with no words

                              birds
                                   appear.

                    (pauses as if waiting—she shrugs)
                              She doesn't believe in words.

CROCODILE-MICHELIN-RHINO *enters somersaulting crumples*
charges crumples in her green-winged crocodile horned rhino dance.
L, R, and TANYA *do not ever notice her. They are not describing her*
ever but speak completely separately from her realm. Here they all
raise their arms in the air as if lifting them to keep out of the way of
someone vacuuming under them—as if to get out of the way of the
CROCODILE-MICHELIN-RHINO *whom they don't see. She dances to*
music track 10, then dance and music end.

L stands in front of the bed in flow and rush of speaking wonder—
without seeing CROCODILE-MICHELIN-RHINO *who's now standing*
still:

L   Hologram of winged crocodile that's
           charging rhino also—at once two
           —swim in the iridescent limb

           they have no senses—everyone

           's low except accept the men pets
           that only hierarchy—mine—

50

halving everything exists
give the rich huge tax breaks

the

form of it (one) is before d void of being
—*is*—rather than one ever being

there

CROCODILE-MICHELIN-RHINO *dances to music track 6.
LEFT-SIDE of the brain, RIGHT-SIDE of the brain, and TANYA keep
their arms up in the air throughout the CROCODILE-MICHELIN-RHI-
NO dance though they never notice her. L gets up on bed. TANYA not
only has her arms in the air, she pauses in a hop of hopscotch and
stands on one foot with the other foot held extended backwards as
if she is skating while she as Patty Hearst still holds her AK47. Dance
and music end. Then CROCODILE-MICHELIN-RHINO stands still in
their midst.*

TANYA *utters wonder as if that is logic of undoing pain of redefinition:*

TANYA   not in terms of *one*—rather than
                   one ever being—is/was mold being
                            redefined and redefined—by
                   outside has interpreted one back to one
                   self in the instant of the actions one is
                                        and/in
                   (*then, only*) one's movements are separate
                                        from being

R *answers TANYA, explaining:*

R   The physical body is separate, alongside, even in
                                 or because one's

hallucination standing the physical body is outside
others loved
in continual double of opposites, solitary free
                                        center
one's physical body is
without language—has no language beside the left side
and the right side no other existence than alive
—not between them either.

TANYA continues in sincere innocence, without appearing to notice R:

Hell or physical bliss space
without words
as
if vomiting the
outside from one in
side
out iridescent one
                        place

L standing on bed:

L   My friend
        —hit by the van—
        thinks it
        's violent
        though

R standing on tea table, simple in bliss—present:

R   she would not need
        to
             try to be
        inside her motions
              do
        ing these—while doing so
             for
        there's no sense of that
        now   —she *is* these.

CROCODILE-MICHELIN-RHINO without music does one rush of the rhino/crocodile charging, crumpling, somersaulting. Then she runs off stage.

L climbs down from bed and begins walking around as if pearl-puking mulls:

L   they mocked our gen

        eration the one again
        st war *for*
        justice—one rebel
        led, as if that were immature
        of us in living—seen as—by
        pundits who're blood leeches
(redundant)   ours locked in struggle with
        the other
        side—as if only *our* stagnant fight
—now   the new has passed to
        a different, free view not locked

in this shown
by The Vote, they're saying

(R gets down from tea table and says casually to L:)

R   though our gen voted
          the new in too

TANYA gets on bed, sits cross-leg on bed and fluffs up pillow around
herself to get comfortable while she talks:

TANYA   the actions one *is*   /in
          then (that one is *only*) are separate from one
          —in them redefining one *to* one?—
          one has fallen out of one's own
                                        is not in
          motions (that) *are* one
          —is that it (that's their/destroying one)?
                              I don't remember—

                  This complex of actions/cycle is gone
                      —the pundits say—good!

*L walking around says to audience, as if she is reading script she's
been told to say at the same time as describing action she herself is
in. Words are spoken in the way they are seen, in the order in which
they appear, rather than altering pronunciation of the word by what it
is later known to be:*

              L   that is,
                  the pundits mock our gen

54

for rebel   ling (he says)

L screws up her face wondering   —reveling?—

as to the meaning of the words   ours seen as locked in fight

"rebel"   "ling"   *only*   puny   having been

against war etc in our eration

gen

L explains the words she's just uttered:
Words are spoken in the way they are seen, in the order in
which they appear, rather than altering pronunciation of the
word by what it is later known to be.

TANYA says this with tender details:

TANYA   gen

tle   be outside

cycle

ing   bicycle   ing

they say—the new is—*now*

R begins to hop hopscotch on invisible lines on the
floor while she says leeches as gorgeous puking:

R   pundits are

blood leeches (redundant) who

've   spent their lives packaging

others' live actions to fit be falsified the same

mold/frame—corpse

TANYA asks L and R:
TANYA   the two parts of the brain

being   the outside's

inside?

L answers, happy:

L   The crowd
             weeps for joy as
             no one had this
             view hope
    of one as them ever before
                 they're a crowd having
                 joy by virtue
                 of that at once

R corroborates L, happy:

R   regardless
            of any future actions
            —*is it*

L walking in circles speaks angrily to herself who is then the ventrilo-quist, who pukes the inside:

L   man in black robes imitated by ventriloquist/moi:
        "The trouble with you
                      is
        you take what you do/
        you see/
        as what *it*/*is*
        what (outside) *is*/is being
        (in/as—*you also* there)
        and that as *then* (only)—it *is*
        —whereas I *don't*" he says
        "I keep these separate."

CROCODILE-MICHELIN-RHINO wearing flapping black robe reenters and does brief dance to music track 6, an abstracted sense of imitating man starving as attempting to eat at invisible plates on the floor but can't get food into his throat.

R gets back up onto bed, holds her arms up in the air as if to keep out of the way of a vacuum cleaner but never sees or looks in the direction of the dancing CROCODILE-MICHELIN-RHINO there. Dance and music end. R's gorgeous puking:

> R   dis/hell/bliss space
>   without words
>   as
>   if vomiting the
>   outside from the one in
>   side
>   out iridescent one.

TANYA sitting on bed holds her arms up to keep out of the way of the motion as if getting up as someone vacuums under one but never looks in the direction of, never sees, the CROCODILE-MICHELIN-RHINO who stands still:

> TANYA   but he can't get one bite
>   in—or vomiting invisible outside

L sits in small child's chair looking benignly smiling out at audience, doesn't see CROCODILE-MICHELIN-RHINO:

> L   If we only exist in injury
>   and

winged swim in bloody
iridescent limb
corpse—two
not stagnant
the two sides of the brain
(she cups ear)   here outside—hear?—is
inside/one in infinite
relation the
inside outside *then?*

R wades around on bed with sea-legs yet coughs black bile. The performers never shout—except when TANYA shouts the train whistle:

R   The Man in Black Robes
coughs black bile
He *thinks* the present—one's—
should not be *what* one's doing

—is—not *what* one's doing
(doing/seeing/thinking)   *then!*

               or *ever!*

L still sitting in small child's chair, sincerely embracing the absent friend:

L   Usually
              embracing generous and brave,

my friend—showing signs
of cynicism reverses negatively
   —hit by a van—she   (and if)

all stupid and low
there is no base.

R standing on bed, encouraging L, implying the implications are favorable:

R   Yet embracing generous and brave—
         indicates—   *she gestures openly as to open space*
         a future?

TANYA who has been sitting on the bed gets off and stands on small child's chair says the black bile:

TANYA   Look, that's *nothing*! supposedly not free
                 another, a different friend—no, *not*
                 friend—higher than one/them (that other says)
         as part of oneself being merely a bully one merely
         imagined (her a) friend, that one
                 —hasn't been hit by a van—
         sees people low venal bullies *hates*
                 them—appears to occur
                                  transformed (*from*)
                 event of being next to/near/to the many
                 those hers dying rending mortal rends

CROCODILE-MICHELIN-RHINO in black robes runs off stage.
R gets off bed, begins hopscotch, looks at TANYA, says dryly:

         R   Raves is "vision"
         supposedly not free   hers
                 gives it validity
                 driven by hers
                 dying mortal
         s   ity rends

TANYA standing on small child's chair explains to the air, staggering her words as if as such the words find out clarity. She announces the title, then speaks the vision:

TANYA   The Portal

       the hypocrite who attacks all the
       people as venal and murderers she's a god says
              having suffered more than any people—
       (their country) who're (their) dying amongst weeping
       bombed—she— "all men will not exist in the future"
              —The Causes: if any LOOK, they're "mean"—
       she says—hates anyone with money so strips the coat
       off any back and celebrating this rends mortal   s
       —to seize theirs—driven by hers/dying she   for
       (she's also) old—(rends) mortal   s *for/as* the remainder
       of—re-*MOVES*—her/their life rends starving *being*
                                 rending
                    as such.

R explains to TANYA:

R   The customs
       of our/their commun
       ity don't actually mirror
       the law—ever—which she knew
       /knows—yet then uses the law
       to get everything away
       from one as/in that—community
              from it

                    the dense
                    light
                    winged box
                    to kill

CROCODILE-MICHELIN-RHINO *runs in wearing black robes that*
flap open showing crocodile-rhino, comes forward fast in front of video
of herself in same dance fast-forwarded at faster speed than danced
in real-time. Music is track 7. Dance and music end. CROCODILE-
MICHELIN-RHINO *sits on floor center back.*

      R stands on one foot, the other leg held raised backward in
      midst of hopscotch game speaks fast urgent flow facing in
      other direction does not see CROCODILE-MICHELIN-RHINO:

R   comes
        forward at once fast forwards himself while he
        stopping the mouths of others—tries to—eat
                        starving, illusion of only his 'get it in'
        at the plates—but he can't—hologram of winged
        crocodile at the time of charging   *same* rhino
        rhino's time crumples—can't get it down—
        charges crumples dissolving

TANYA *standing on child's chair pukes gorgeously with a perfectly*
normal expression—mimes oaring, at the word:

TANYA   *vomiting invisible outside:*

                    don't have
                    stories
                form/stories form

deregulation
corporate here oar
not illustrating
imitate motions exactly
only

*R still holding hopscotch position with one leg
raised held stationary as if she is skating:*

R   Barbie doll with horns

                      eats

                    moose—

        not illustrate her as *friend* in

        outside *halving* it now only

*CROCODILE-MICHELIN-RHINO sits on floor, still. R gets up on and
stretches out over tea table lying propped on one elbow and thought-
fully reads an imaginary book:*

"You dwell upon yourself too much. That's the trouble. And
that produces a terrible fatigue." "But what else can anyone do,
don Juan?" "Seek and see the marvels all around you. You will get
tired of looking at yourself alone, and that fatigue will make you
deaf and blind to everything else."

*CROCODILE-MICHELIN-RHINO dances briefly to music track 2,
discards black robe while dancing; under it is her as green-winged
crocodile melded as hologram also of Michelin-man, a one-horned
grey rhino. She crumples and charges. Dance and music end.*

L still sitting in child's chair chats in conversational,
hopeful tone:

L   our bloody iridescent
                limb
        at rhino's time that crumples
        charges is rolling winged crocodile
                in air

R lying on the tea table looks aside from her book, says mildly to L:

R   You'd have to think
        what they/he/think/thinks is important

L looks up at R and addresses her emphatically:

L   I've always constructed
                everything
      on the basis of what
                everyone
                    thinks
      at once.

TANYA still standing on child's chair, sarcastically:

TANYA   You just *thought*
                    it was
              (what you think)
                (she says)
        "because you are a bully"
("you pushed me into [BLANK] speaking to")
         "into/knowing you
              even"

R stands up on tea table and holds position on one foot as if in hopscotch game. In quoted remarks, she's dryly imitating herself and others speaking at once:

R   Obliterate society

           and then—it will begin.

                    "That's just *you*."
                    "(Right.)" or
                    "(I don't believe that any more.)"

                    R scrambles off table top

L stands up from sitting in child's chair, stretches:

L   because that's what *it* is
                    the whole/hole
           winged crocodile emerges from
                    it at once.

                    TANYA sarcastic:

           TANYA   You *think*

CROCODILE-MICHELIN-RHINO dances to music track 7, somersaulting crumples charges crumples. Video of her in fast-forward crumple-charges is seen behind her. She races forward and then back and forward again in both images. Suddenly, the fast-forward image is slowed to be at the same timing as her real-time (now suddenly slow) dance (though maybe not at the same place in it). Music ends, video continues in silence. CROCODILE-MICHELIN-RHINO is still.

TANYA still standing on child's chair:

TANYA   hierarchy is being

                          outside

            only   ,   *exists*

R standing on one foot on tea table speaks in gorgeous bile facing left, away from CROCODILE-MICHELIN-RHINO whom she never sees:

R   Billows of the crumpling   MP
                         is them
      rhino in green-winged crocodile
      hologram floats in limb
      s   of iridescent crowd   s one
      pressed into them

Video ends.

L, doing in-place stretching exercises, says casually:

L   No matter how violent MR
                        acts
      bullying and hollering, harrowing
            crowd/me/so *man*
     . starving
      trying to eat at the plates fast forwarding him
    self to them embraces MR a man to take his place

, since he can't do it, rather than a woman—he's seen
              while he butts rafting winged crocodile
                      hologram of rhino and Barbie
                      doll with horns eats

TANYA walks to bed, scrambles up on it and begins jumping
on it: she looks at something at random, points at random:

TANYA   there

will be no change
negatively reverses *there*
                              everything
unharmed miraculously—hit by a van—
                      she sees

R changes to other foot, standing on tea table: fast-flow-speaking gor-
geous puking:

R   control of others—stop their
                  thought—they might succeed
         he fast forwards him   self-hologram
         flowing winged crocodile now rhino swim in
         blood in limb of corpse floats up
         these—an instant later—he's seen
                  hologram   of eating ones
         at the plates (on the floor) one's present/
         any seeing/and actions are unrelated
         of oneself to occurrence at all outside rhino
         crumples charges crumples in winged ripples

R stamps working out the kinks from standing too long on one foot:

R   Get it straight

TANYA urging R on to work out the kinks in her foot—as TANYA shouts enthusiastically, she stamps on the bed and holds up her arm to grip an imaginary pull-string, as if on a train:

TANYA WuWuWuWuWuWuWuWuWuWuWuWuWuWuWu
           GoStop!
           GoStop!

                TANYA   they wave

                (after TANYA says this they all wave at unseen
                others in audience—not at CROCODILE-
                MICHELIN-RHINO lying on floor whom they
                never see)

L gets up and stands on a child's chair speaks as man in black robes, ventriloquist, and herself at once, on flood:

        L   Ventriloquist for man in black robes speaks
                sometimes misspeaks/omits to program

                    Odile and Hour

                I have contempt
                    for people—he says—
                who're in desperation
                they're not there yet—
                in physical pain rhino

hologram of green-winged croc

pauses, looks at empty spot—not at crocodile-Michelin-rhino who is
lying on back center floor:

odile charges crumples
rolls in the air charging waft

s our bloody iridescent limb

R   *can*
        descent
        in
        mid mesas?

TANYA turns aside stamping her feet on the bed speaking to herself
as some other's fury utters title:

TANYA   The Portal

        Turns to her suddenly/after twenty-five years—
"Because you're a bully, I accepted [BLANK]—you bullied me
        to imagine/ think *you* a friend—your stupid
        [BLANK] /is worthless" "why didn't you say any
        thing then?"—"Yet (nevertheless) I'll take your
money—and everything you've done's ugly/it's ugly to me"
                                    (takes it anyway)

From standing on the child's chair, L embodying someone else gets up
onto tea table with R:

L The man (black robes), unable to eat, starving, seek
s control of people "I have contempt
for people who are like this/other
    thing—they've come for advice
—the one I'm saying," he says "so it's difficult
to say it."—Not theirs— the winged crocodile eats the
    people's
    other's
feet. They hang their feet in the water.

CROCODILE-MICHELIN-RHINO stands and runs off stage.

*R having been standing on one foot, puts both feet on tea table,
speaking to herself:*

   R   (coming back to her senses)

      I didn't mean "Obliterate society" in this way

      though did intend vomiting invisible outside

        on the trains

*R gets down from tea table using child's chair. R stands on the chair. L
stands on the tea table, embodies man in black robes unable to eat:*

   L   The Ones Who Come for Advice

       I tell them

       what they're

       to think

(as what

they're doing
—to *do*—outside's action

—what it *is*
they can't see—for

if they *do*/it/are that's them

that's mixing the two
that's incorrect.

TANYA speaks casually as explanation; in altered tone, passage is different from before:

TANYA   He thinks the present—one's—
               should not be *what* one's doing
               coughing bile, laughing—whatever
               —*is*—not *what* one's doing
               (doing/seeing/thinking)   *then!*

                                        or *ever!*

L serenely turns on tea table:

L   But seen in real space
           compare to water-stream on mesas red gorges of stairs
           the brain breaking through to dream
           this sight/site is real place, space:

L lies down on tea table:

L   The *man*—
        lounging—on—lying on his—one elbow
        is/was propped on
        it in the vast green gold grass plain on
        above/*depth* purple air gold mountains reverse
                                  float above
        him dark indigo purple separates by him
        stretched beneath standing-horse in the gold grass by
        beside the lying   *man*
                who is in the grass *seen* lying alone.

TANYA   with one's *own*
                eyes—reverts
            to him—dis hell bliss

R steps down from child's chair and begins walking in circles that are
the paradise:

R   She would not need
        to
                try to be
        inside her motions
                do
        ing these—while doing so
                for
        there's no sense of that
        now   she *is* these
                before

If all
are low
birds
no
hierarchy
exists.

L   The crowd
       weeps for joy as
       no one had this
       has view hope
of one as them ever before
       they're a crowd having
       joy by virtue
       that at once

               regardless
               of any future actions
               —is it

TANYA is doing stretches standing on the bed. She puffs:

TANYA   the other
         as if she pushes
         in space too
         —imitates—
         outside
         exists
         two

L lying blissfully on tea table:

L   If we only
          exist in
          —injury—
          —winged swim in bloody
                iridescent limb—
          corpse in   it.

R as if imitating L—could be either mocking or sincere:

R   "Not recycling
          breaks through
          to a dream
          as I'm walking
          toward them
          in (through) the horses
          they won't hurt me
                in it"

L stands up on tea table, gives logical as passionate painful account
staggered:

L   Accidentally O.D.ed
                The Brain Recycled on
                    a Hallucinogen Would sometimes
                Break Through To a Dream outside:

This dream occurred only once though

        the horses pour

                ing
on the crack that's where the billion-tiered
stairs-sides of the red mesa meet they're

galloping from the opening onto the crack midst
vast ranges of other red mesa-gorges

                              everywhere the
outside red billion stairs between which on the crack I
walk(ed) toward the opening,
          of crack, through which innumerable
horses are galloping toward me the stream of them
          opening passes me,
          they don't trample or touch me
          "they won't hurt me" is thought.

TANYA sits on bed with her legs dangling off the end of bed, that's
facing the audience. She begins her own simultaneous world:

TANYA   Years earlier (than what?
                              —than now)
          while in real space

                              sweeping behind me (seen from)
                    (a being) dragged by a horse
                              is (sees) a forest—downed—
                                        in a hurricane
                                        beside/by me
                    trees fly and float ahead

L lies down on tea table again, propped on one elbow in the rush of
TANYA'S flowing world:

          L   awed
                    horse-riding
                    ahead
                    produces
              real space event of

others years later
here

TANYA   The Trains

    I wanted—to *be*
    —a hobo—my boyfriend
    —my to—hop the trains—*we*
    will dress as men—for protection
    I tell him/but he
    says to me I don't think
    you can pass—
                —everything—(is)

R imitates herself by suddenly (after trying to remember how) resum-
ing position of standing on one foot, the other leg held extended
backward in air:

R   the brain
        recycles—only—is
                from
        something happening
        the *outside*
                it
        is nothing in itself?

TANYA still sitting dangling her feet off the bed:

    TANYA   She doesn't believe in words

L while lying on tea table, as she's propped on one elbow—in the
midst of speaking the man in the grass, she re-writes that space?

L   Compare her real space to my seeing this in real space
then only *seen*—seen now—:

A man—
lounging—on—lying on his—one elbow
is propped on
it in the vast green gold grass plain on
above/*depth* purple air gold mountains reverse
                              float
below, him dark indigo purple separates by/beside him
stretched beneath—horse stands—in the gold grass by
        the lying   *man*
who is in the grass seen lying alone.

TANYA sitting on bed says accusingly:

TANYA   See! It's altered! Anyway, is this *all?*
"You haven't done anything *for* me," the now/not
ever/ friend/the woman said.

*L lying luxuriously on tea table, unheeding TANYA, utters a
robotic stream:*

              L   The crowd weeping
                       with joy—entranced
                       there is change

              L   The Vote—pundits
                       who follow it
                       just sit
may refer to TANYA   blood leeches/redundant who

make the same frame
as before, stagnant
corrupt it
filling up the time.

Behind them on back wall a video of green-winged CROCODILE-
MICHELIN-RHINO is being played in silence (during the following
speeches), her dance in reverse, backwards faster than real time. Video
stops before reversed image of dancing CROCODILE-MICHELIN-
RHINO disappears.

R stands on both feet in front of tea table — says calmly:

R   saying our gen
                  in space
                  just
          fight as if locked with others
immature but old—is gone—
didn't we want of that? war etc
          gone? our gen
eration —as if just *seeing* as   that is
          automatic? engorged   —is gone
                  good!

TANYA stands on bed:

TANYA   individuals seen in
                  the crowd weep
                  with joy—

TANYA is outside's gorgeous puking:

TANYA   I rode horse   back
                      the horse trying to scrape me off
                      its back through the tree

                      s whole forest standing
                      no longer

                      —having been—downed
                      in the hurricane
                      flaps invisible before us (horse
                      and I were)   riding
                      the horse drags me through the
                      huge forest brushing me.

                                      Looks
                          As if they don't believe me.

Video of winged CROCODILE-MICHELIN-RHINO in reverse stops.

L gets up from lying position on tea table, stands on the table, utters seeing and gorgeous puking space to the audience in it. She announces the title, then speaks the vision:

L   Two

    We (two people) standing on a cliff in the sky on sea
                              two flying ahead
  land/sing/stamp *"Come on!"* jetting cliff then as they
  peer into sky to sing the others in—the others don't appear
                      —yet—the two take off ahead

—at once the green-blue-glittering migrating come in
while they dive and ascend equally into and from the black-
red they rose on flower-flow-plateau of black-red lava flower-flow
bed innumerable come flying in flower   s into it equally
green-blue-glittering air-borne diving and ascending at once
the migrating Vs come in by the two people standing on cliff in
the sky on sea

L gets down from tea table and walks to place in front of bed while
TANYA speaks standing on bed hurling quietly:

TANYA   The racing moon
                            past
               the trains pass
               the yellow war ribbons all tied
                            around trees
               by the tracks

               The people thought.

               This was sentiment.

R begins to hop hither and thither:

R   then very irritating

               People think too
               that   candidate, Barbie doll
               with horns—just because she didn't win—
                            is gone   (when she isn't)

L standing in front of bed, looking at audience says calmly:

L   A dear friend man having died   the other
        man says the center to be filled only by
        close friends—but/and—he does not allow
             anyone to enter the center

                              so the center is empty

*R from hopping here and there gets up on tea table. R stretches
across the tea table lying propped on one elbow and sees herself in
gorgeous puking as of others:*

R   The actions one *is*   /in
             /*then* (one is that *only*) are separate from one
             —in their redefining one *to* one?—
             one has fallen out of—is no longer *in*—one's own
                  motions (that) *are* one

                                    being

             —is that it?—I don't remember

TANYA gets down from bed and asks quietly:

      TANYA   Are they not
                         the marvels—spill over
                         vomiting invisible outside

L   —Suddenly—
        words would disappear
        —not omitted even—re-*MOVE*
        the words from the space *there*
             the space was/is there

80

R draped on tea table, L and TANYA stand. They pause, are still,
while—beginning at the word "suddenly"—CROCODILE-MICHELIN-
RHINO runs in and begins dancing to music track 10 while video
of green-winged CROCODILE-MICHELIN-RHINO dancing is being
played fast in reverse. CROCODILE-MICHELIN-RHINO dances, then
runs off stage. Video of dance in reverse plays with music until dancer
on video disappears.

THE END

A PAIR / ACTIONS ARE ERASED / APPEAR

A NOH PLAY

For Tracy Grinnell—for the pleasure of working together

LEFT-SIDE speaker (L) is the left side of the brain, a young woman dressed in a slinky black dress. RIGHT-SIDE speaker (R) is the right side of the brain, a young woman dressed in a colorful dress of purple, green, red. OUTSIDER-RENEGADE (OR) is a young woman dressed in ordinary, simple skirt and blouse. She moves freely always independent, whereas RIGHT-SIDE speaker and LEFT-SIDE speaker tend to stay close to each other and converse with each other. MR is a man dressed in plates of grey (maybe large type of bubble wrap) covered with tufts of green moss as the green-moss-covered-hanging-two-toed-sloth; he also has a grey horn on his forehead (horn of the simultaneously charging rhino, as hologram of sloth and rhino).

MR uses a stepladder (which is sometimes also used by the women as a stool), and also a rope that's hanging from the ceiling, to climb up to a brown shelf (a branch) where he draws up his legs and arms in front of him presenting his back to the audience sack-like as the hanging sloth on the branch. When MR unfolds and climbs down assuming his rhino manifestation, he crumples and charges, crumples and charges gracefully and as soundlessly as possible. In one scene he wears binoculars around his neck.

The text is to be spoken as casual conversation, though one person may be speaking possibly attitudes and gestures of several people at once. As such, a speaker may undercut or enforce her own opinions and imitate other people's attitudes and their speaking simultaneously. Pairs of poems are merely demonstrations visually on the page of the right side and the left side of the brain as these may be different but of equal strength simultaneously. Where there are paired passages, the left side is read vertically first, then the right side is read vertically.

The stage has here and there at higher and lower levels billboard-like signs (on sticks attached to the floor or wires attached to the ceiling) painted as pink folds: the right and left sides of the brain with its sections but also suggestive of clouds or floating jewels. LEFT-SIDE speaker, RIGHT-SIDE speaker, and OUTSIDER-RENEGADE all at one time or another stand with their heads/faces protruding above a floating brain or, depending on the height of the billboard-jewel-brain, their trunks and heads seeming to stem from the floating brains. They stroll amidst the floating brains casually, gracefully, sometimes imitating imaginary physical actions (such as an imaginary serve of the ball in tennis without a ball or racket being present) always as if these actions are performed by a ghost (though the person is still alive) or as though the actions are ghost actions/past of the living person.

L and R stand even with each other on left and right sides of the stage separated, each standing with their head or head and trunk above a floating pink brain (that is, there are two floating brains on the left and on the right sides and here and there in the space); OR stands front stage, her head protruding from a pink floating brain or jewel. She speaks dreamily:

OR   now
          dreamed
          I hit the sun
          last night
          with my hand

L   A man
    inviting   R   to
    to   collaborate (arrives in the room)
                                  on—?
    his glistening black   flies in   (he's in)
    robes—seen in the moon   enters
    the room   lies in   furious
        is blinded to himself

First L and then R sing their passages. They both have a balmy, blissful attitude

L   man
    inviting   R   I
    to   collaborate
    arrives in   the room
    on
    his   glistening black

```
                           (in)
       robes—seen in      the moon
       enters             the room
       flies in           ZOOM  S
       furious
```

OR speaks the title of her speech, the subject being hell yet she has a blissful tone:

```
OR                         Hell Dis
              Held on a leash by robed
              in black who,    alone,
              condones, compliments
                           him
              oblivious to though describing
              the rage hollering I'll
              squash all flat how
              in mid life the people trapped?
                           by his
              largesse, behest/alone
```

L and R move away from their respective floating brains/billboards. They stroll slowly amidst these floating jewels. R strolls to the stepladder and casually sits down on it.

```
L        a man
         (to me)
         "Rebel" as action
         another
         said
         "Collaboration doesn't work"
```

when at ease, resting

not what he meant

R   invites

to collaborate
having done so
"The thing about collaboration is"
in
the sense
calm when it isn't
working (isn't)
"Collaboration doesn't *work*"

L casually stoops to pick an imaginary posy, speaking matter-of-factly:

L   MR insists on only holding onto money
       and with (that occurring) the humble suffering
       —*then*
       having authority is the nature of *his*
                                there
       (the other) who has put that (with MR) in place.

L straightens and speaking indicates horizontal expanse:

actions' half-
sha
dows that
link up
horizontal
ly at

87

at places
their sides   *OR is front stage; she begins to stroll:*
touch
are beside   OR   inside
each other   work is in
there objects/   the day
sides sweep   drops
                         shooting
                         star is
                         at the bottom

OR   I first   mountains walk
       noticed   everywhere
       mountains walk   their
       walking   edges meet
       on water   horizontal at
       of a huge river   once mountains everywhere

OR speaks the single poems, vertically; then she repeats, singing across horizontally, omitting "I" in the first line and "of" in the line 6 "a huge river." She's expansive as if she's Doris Day:

L   we're   OR   woman
       in a savannah   can
       everywhere   di   date
       wrecked cars   foists
       hang in the air   her religion
       splashes   on us
                                  as if hers *were*

L	black	R	fans
	glistening		
	in		the
	perfume		ed
	night		night
	he flies in		
	roiling		in
	the		glistened
	he's		he's
	robes (black)		_____ (*pauses suspended*)
		OR	people
	(*pauses suspended*)		listened to

| L | of authority | R | *assumed!* |

OR bounces an imaginary tennis ball lightly in her hand and serves it hitting it with an imaginary tennis racket, her action as if playing tennis is done by a ghost perceived by a living person.

OR speaks the title of her words as if casually inside and outside of a dream that's hell and paradise:

OR   Alone Dis Hell

    Is the holder being backed
    by the authority of black
    robes as traps others who are good
    while to sustain one hollering
    holding onto the money of charity berates beats the
    entrapped there shall not be charity it doesn't
    make money is not good business
    he could give—the humble suffering when the man is

                                        all at the guidance of that
               authority is that/(alone)

                         Unraveling action—alone
                         seemingly magic cows bowed
                         on bright green—are really there
                         grass feeding the white cows
                         appear passed future

                                    They appear by that action

                                    passed future

_____

They speak the tiny parts of words to catch an interior shape that is
of the space, not simply those words:

L   work that inside   R   causes
         —has the quali   ity of—
         ty—of—one
         to see   oneself—
         having—   of
         "rebelling"
         itself

L and OR begin to play an imaginary tennis game with each other,
very gracefully minimal gestures:

L   that is
         thought—see

```
ing      itself
         by
         "rebelling"
see it   beside                    OR      from
         itself                                    itself?

                                   (slight pause)

                                   work
                                   in/is
                                    "rebelling"
                                   shooting
                                   star
                                   —in night—
                                   —in day
                                   ap pear
```

```
            R      holds   out
                   her     hand
```

L utters the title "Alone" of her speaking. She's both sardonic and as if comparing her subject in space with her imaginary tennis game, hitting of the tennis ball:

L   Alone

MR at the benevolence and so authority of black
robes hollers in mid life not only
for the leeway and holding money back a bottle
neck to everyone but as if I'll squash all flat
as if sits on the houses of the humble yet
on a leash held by the authority of robes
                                        alone.

*R, who has been sitting on the stepladder, rises and earnestly
addresses L:*

R For
   being
   alert to
   memories
   and present
   as emotions
    any
   is if real-ly low,
   incorrect
   being so are
   actually
   invisible.

   No present existing,
   in fact.

Individual Beings

Being so are
actually invisible
in mid life
and as infants.

L ceases her game, turns and looks at R and answers:

L hold out her hand
  re   R "she
  ferring to   was
  nothing there   beside
        herself"
          from
          herself

                              immediately
                                 de
                                parts

L says with disgust: *OR speaks serenely without*
                              looking at either L or R:

L   I'm sick of innocence   OR   the two parts
                                            of the brain
                                            equal at once
         seen   race
         it appears   together always
                                               seemed
                                            in conflict
                                            or (oar) serene.

---

*While the L and R converse, and OR is in her own realm, all without
ever seeing MR, MR-hanging-sloth-charging-rhino enters runs
skittering climbs up on rope to branch and hangs briefly with legs
up lump-sack on branch then runs again as charging rhino down on
knees stumbles up again charging. He is graceful making as little
noise as possible. He runs with binoculars tied around his neck and
occasionally looks through them behind him as if watching others
bombed as he runs away but occasionally seeming to draw himself
up hunched as the sloth (who is covered with green moss because he
is so motionless).*

*L muses to herself, unaware of MR and not speaking to either R or
OR:*

L   Remembering one's first I.Q. test at the age before
         reading—though green hanging sloth (so motionless

green moss has grown on it) bursts in a charging
rhino—when one's trying to concentrate—asked
What is the left hand?—easily, I extended the left hand.

*MR is continuing to charge and crumble, hunch as sloth and charge
as rhino, invisible to the women who discuss someone else, the man
in black robes:*

L   while
           the
           robes of authority   R   in-robes
           is racist
                 one   regarding
           people   *his* self
           against an   authority
other   people   —he's pitted
           unrelated   entirely
           to each   unrelated
                other   other peoples
           he's—
           imagines isn't?   to be racist
           —is to show—   to *one*
           not is—"*not*"—to—*be* racist?   people now.

          R   He says
          "We should cover up
          no one will know the order"
          —of the floating jewels—
          one enters and leaves
          "otherwise, we'll look stupid."

L   baffling
     me   *Inquiring, wanting a summary:*
     —what does
             his   OR   does *negatively*
     being racist to   regarding
     the Japanese   Japanese have—
     have to   do
     with   having *good*
     his— *good*   attitude—in *him*
view toward   —toward—
     people   an   other
     —*who're*   people not his
     Black *here?*   who in the past   *from*
                                  Africa—are here?

            R   move it
                 into
                         that space
                 not *out*

L   immediately   R   if there is
                             no
     he takes   causation—
     —the   in this if
authority-as-robes   causation is
     —this   lifted
     as   *look*—there's
     literal   horizontal motions?
     thwart
     ing

95

of
authority—by
her

_____

OR   forward—

Though MR is doing his dance as sloth-charging-rhino and now
looking back behind him with binoculars tied around his neck, OR
does not see him. She speaks spitting the words gorgeously:

OR   MR a hologram of supine two-toed—he's so motionless
        he's green moss-covered sloth hanging in the midst of a
        charging rhino—Halliburton (or someone) supposed to
        reconstruct Iraq at war's end (but doing nothing, pocketing the
                                        money)—
        charges warring between the green sloth as charging rhino—
        and to feed US troops engineers
        dining outside at once long lines to eat
        being more convenient financially though exposes the soldiers
        en masse to attack ratta-tat-tat ratta-tat bomba
        bomba. bomba. bomba. Ba-boomb. Ba-boomb.
                                spoken as if Spanish accent

L spits out the words gorgeously: *R concurs indignant:*

L   woman believes she   R   "I'm"—as if place
                        wins   d   ahead
        in—someone believing   of other actions
        they're a close *friend*   "a hypocrite
        while *real*   *ly* her   and a coward" she
        not (caring) for them   *said—would—do (so)*
                is a space ahead?   to   win some

_____

96

OR's actions of playing an imaginary tennis game have been transformed into her having an imaginary butterfly net with which she is bagging butterflies lightly loping catching them:

OR   Charity is not good business you don't take money
                                  out of the bank should be
      run to profit—if you're losing it, you can't
      operate—Have everyone arrive to eat at once
      serve them once—together in the same place
                          everyone,
      they're a target. Get it? You don't give it away.

      Why is china called china?
      eating cake on the china—
      drinking tea from the china—
      the white silken creased necks
      wattles of the white humps
      on the cattle as same oar or
      opposite   drinking on the bright
                    green.

OR   the white silken creased humps
               wattles of the cattle—oar
                        on the bright
                        green

MR returns to the stepladder and rises to the shelf (branch) where he folds his limbs in front of himself, his plates (or rhino with patches of green moss of sloth) hanging down slightly from shelf, his back to audience, he becomes still again. They are all thinking privately in their separate realms without contact with each other. OR finally articulates a middle space that they have been making unaware of this:

*L, R, and OR are in the same space almost touching but not seeing
each other:*

L   half-

                not herd
                flower
     ing s oar plants
            fold
   and expand horizon
   tal the outside beside inside

     sweep   R   by
     in   taking
     horizontal   place
     swatches

                      OR   low
                              animals

                              re
                              bell
                              ing

R   baffling

                me
     —what
     views
     the Japanese
     to do
     with *not*
     having
     toward (people)
     here?

```
OR      conversion across
                horizontally
         the  outside beside
                          inside
         alters/is midst
         it          (no view)
```

OR, addressing R, speaks the exact actions that MR as green sloth-rhino made in the past, a past that at the time had no words:

```
OR      MR-hanging-sloth-charging-rhino runs skittering
        climbs up on rope to branch and hangs briefly with legs
        up lump-sack on branch then runs again as charging rhino
        down on knees stumbles up again charging. He runs
        with binoculars tied around his neck and occasionally looks
        through them behind him as if watching others bombed as
        he runs away. Ba-boomb. boomba.
                             last words as if Spanish accent
```

```
R       Because we hear in the middle. No, maybe because
        we "don't hear in the middle"?
```

*L mulls without paying any attention
to the others:*

```
L                     Imagining she's
         a friend—from years ago
         now she says—"I only even
         spoke to you because you're
         a bully—you bullied me to
                        know you
```

the same woman seriously
(meaning "singular" and as such
seeming to degenerate by regarding
others as inferior, boasts having the highest
intelligence in her kindergarten class
of a small town.

OR, not listening to L, is still puzzling:

OR   does   his
racism   toward
Japanese

not   *be*
racism toward
        —*forward?*
an
other?

OR   Phenomenal change is being seen bewildering as
people's *feelings* also (even not acted upon—or is
acted upon). Bewildering one or seen at once (which
may be the same) leads to there being *no* view.

L   "Right." or "Sure Sure"

the whole
state
de (di)
regulated
goes
—state of bliss

R	he says the	OR	plants	lay
	that's only			quiet
	present			in
	being			reconnaissance
	is			oar
	tradition *too*			to each other
	—at once *me*—			flower *ing* plants
	so I'm to be			no organs
	within/as— *that*		except only reproductive
	the outside		they move

---

*L, R, and OR try to hold a space slightly apart from each other
without touching or seeing each other:*

L   woke up
in the
morning
years later
see
is
not/*very*
bright
at all
separate   the sun
(could be son)
S-O-N

       R (*muffled*)   (could be son)

(make it out)

(They both squint ahead looking)

L still squinting cups ear:

L   directly at it hear it is not the same

          Motion takes a long or a short time *seen*

	that is		
	thought—see	R	having
	itself		being produced
	by		or
	rebelling		allowing that
see it	beside		—either—
	itself		at once actual
			moon—
		he enters the room	
		there's a midst	
		a middle	

L, R, and OR try to hold a space slightly apart from each other
without touching or seeing each other:

L	If		
	in	R	this
	illumine		mined
	present		—if
	so—		moving
	there		is
	no		past
	present either		—or
	not		—and ahead

that
is   —if illumined
what   straightforwardness
present *is*   only
—*now*   —*now*

L   In the
          sense that rebelling
          from one's
          (way of) seeing—
          of one's
          own authority in one's seeing
                           even
          if this comes to be—or is the
          particular instance of seeing
                      and any
          way of it occurring in time is always outside
                (is always outside of them)

the way one repeats this
          seeing
even rebelling from one's
seeing (repeating that) is always outside
it   /and them

                  R   Is that good, or bad?

*MR as sloth huddled hanging on branch begins to unfold, climbs
down and as rhino begins to charge fall to his knees charge.*

L   So it becomes the ideal
              (rebelling)

became
but then one is simply
outside seeing
                    —him.
MR holding the money?

OR   At the front of the class at the age before reading
        put out the hand—when asked (in one's first I.Q. test)
                                for the left
        hand—concentrating, though MR sloth in midst of rhino runs in
        stumbling to knees charges stumbles charges—there will be no
                                charity
        —feed them at once in a long line out onto the
        desert—boomba. bomba. rata-ta-ta-ta-ta
                        last words as if Spanish accent

L   they're   OR   I
        in a savannah   —my—
        everywhere   *used*
        wrecked cars   (brain's)   two sides
        hang in the air   to
            out of them   be
        instead of clouds   at   war

                        a   fa   cul   ty
                            —*with me*—

L and R resume discussing, addressing each other directly:

L then he this

                    R starts in

hammering   on the

"Arabs"   —where he

surfaces   hating

saying—that   I'm (he says)

childish I'm   as, immature only,

James Dean in   "rebelling" of

Rebel Without a Cause James Dean in

                   Rebel Without a Cause

OR moves as if scratching her right side/rib cage
with her right knee, monkey-like, or as a dog would scratch:

L not seeing   OR no

—he hadn't—

seen the movie   a forest horse

or reading   tries

—or read—   to scrape me

the book   *off*

                     its   back

L they're in a *savannah*   OR   all

by *wrecked*   cars   actions are

that hang in the savannah   making

where's the middle? the cars outside dropping

    hang *on* the midst   horizon plants

        of its   *air.*   tal shimmer on it

OR is trying to get everything into one space—she continues to
scratch her right rib cage with her right knee while speaking:

<pre>
                    OR   moons cars behavior
                            actions at once
                            not
                            authority
                            ever—too?
        ("not being ever" is also "too")is/are
                            tradition
                            reason cars plants
           tiger spoon words ever and too
                            and sun there
                            with   moon?
</pre>

L and R sarcastically compare two spaces while MR is continuing his
dance:

<pre>
L   "   —/—
        wouldn't be affected
        by this"—he forbade
           others to enter
              the center
        of the room as "for
        close friends"—at
        the death of a friend
           it was empty
        (only)   —"You—
        would be" (affected)
        (by this)
        he forgot to fill the center.
</pre>

R   though,
    James Dean really
             had
    a reason for rebelling
    I
    don't know *why*
    it's   *called*
    Rebel Without a Cause?
    because we can't stand
          causes?

        OR   bring in

L	Then he	R	starts in
	hammering		on the
	"Arabs"	"Arabs"	where he
	surfaces		hating
	saying		I'm
	"childish		"rebelling" of
	James (FLAILS)	James	Dean in
	Rebel Without		*a Cause*

L	he's	R	he
	wanting		revenge
			out
	hammering		the "Arabs"
	for they're		their
	being "murderers"		he says "murderers"
	doesn't hear me		he doesn't hear me

MR spits it out happily and smiling. He speaks as if there is a conversation going between two people spoken aloud only by himself, lifts his voice as a question at the end of sentences with question marks as he cocks his head listening:

MR   Sewers caused all our troubles. The masses in the US... they are slave stock? They are good for nothing but slaves and only when they are used as slaves are they happy?...But we, the decent people, made the mistake of giving them modern housing in the cities where we have our factories? We put sewers in these cities, sewers which extend right down to the workers' quarters? Not content with the work of God, we thus interfere with His will? The result is that the slave stock increases? Had we no sewers...all these Red leaders would have died in their infancy instead of exciting the rabble and causing good blood to flow? When the war is over, we should

(MR) destroy the sewers? After we bombed Iraq, Halliburton didn't repair the sewers!—Take billions (with no bid contracts) from tax payers to repair their sewers!—the people still walk in sewage! Float in rivers of it! See? The perfect birth control for the US is that which God intended us to have? No schools? Sewers are a luxury to be reserved for those who deserve them, the leaders? Leaps in thought, thought shows dementia?

OR enters the same space as MR, she is speaking dreamlike without seeing him who is close by her:

OR   *now*
       dreamed
       I hit the sun
       last night
       with my hand

OR walks floating dreamlike amidst the brain-jewels on sticks. R is awed watching her. MR withdraws and climbs up again onto shelf (branch) where he resumes being a hanging sloth.

OR   any day
           unrelated to
           any
                    other
           when

                    at all *actions*
           things   star radish tea
                    now

R   she's not Amish "Rebel"
                  outside?
          —in—peaceful quilting
          will make one
          outside for them (future)
          to bring—it—*in*
          (get these ap   pear
          —to—
          produce each other)

L   reach   OR   —the—
          out   her   lit tle
                        hand   words
          there s a pear   —fold—
          there appears   —"foal"—
          the outside beside inside

L and R forget about OR who drifts off. L and R begin declaiming to each other:

L   Barbie doll
              candidate
                          LIKES   ignorance (appear s)
              —she thinks/says—she's The People
                          that   *only*
              —ignorance is— The People
                                        with horns

R   Years later
         calls me
         to come in
         vites me
         here
         his talk   to
         others: "scientists   are
         stealing the blood
          of the Indians in
         the Amazon," a movie
         —he accuses me of   it's
         a hoax I know about
                              but
         he won't believe me

L   behind is   OR   to practice
         in horizontal   only
         swatches   *present*
         same at day   *being*
                                          is
                                          only tradition
                                          at once

so I'm to be
within/as *that*
only *now*.

OR scratches with her right knee round and
round on her right rib cage:

L   He would never *think.*   OR   dragging
                                        me
          (pause)   under boughs of trees
                                the horse wanted to
                                "tree me"

L   *now*
    never
     here
    my *self*
    as only
    in day is
            light
    chasing

R   "and
    still,
    it
    moves"

MR as green-sloth-rhino moves, unfolds briefly on branch
allows his legs to hang off shelf-branch.

OR   con
        cealed
        appear
        to be chasing
        each other
        cause it?

L   Yes. Not long later
        he confides
        "I used to be
        a   racist. A man
        taking me aside, says

        not to be racist I saw it
        and learned—(not to be)."
        I'm baffled—
        did
        he hear this   *before*
        or *after*   I'd
        pointed this out re
            garding
        the Japanese   and
        unrelated to /then
        my rebelling *from*
        my thought

R   "but *then* someone—
    the man said not to be
    —I saw it and learned
    from the man
        out regarding—not
    to be a racist"—is
    the other man   before

or after—   not
in—our collaboration,
when   the word
"rebelling" incurred
his

                    contempt?

L   There are *no* people?

                    OR is summarizing for clarification:

          OR   he decides
                      to
                      out-of-the-blue
                      go after
                      this person—
                      neither Japanese
                      nor Black—*and*
                      as   he
                      goes after the
                      Japanese too

                      R   *then*
                                  he's
                                  not
                                  mentioning
                                  me
                                  to me

          OR   having
                    being produced

```
                                     or
                                     allowing that
                                     —either—
                                     at once
```

(They say the word "[BLANK]" with sprightly sarcasm.)

```
L      woke up        R              up
                at                   at
       morning              morning he's
                see                      in
       he's so                      that
       regard             he could not hear
   s      women he        or even remember.
       me      at all
       I'm [BLANK]        We're [BLANK]
```

```
L      now
       we're (so) [BLANK]
       so        the other
       man tells him
       not to be racist   OR      the
                                  government
       he doesn't even            is going
       remember      me
       saying                     to give
                    (it)
       he didn't hear me          antelopes
```

OR addresses L & R:

OR   And he doesn't remember any of this occurring—?!

OR pauses, waits until L who is looking at her and has eye-contact smiles, at first tentatively, then beams. R is looking face forward at audience but relaxes at this point and smiles also:

          OR   Actions are erased
                 they   *appear*
              to be chasing each other

                      R   The other side
                            of here is

                                  [BLANK]?

                      Yes

L   *now*
    outsider-renegade
    my self
    joining *then*
    in day is
        light
    chasing

L   he   OR   I
    sneers   used
    at 'free'   to   *be*
    being   at   war
    the   (pronounced 'thee')   with equal

present actions		(brain's) sides =	faculty
		my	self

R   shooting fish at the bottom of the day dropping star
falling shoots in the day—ap pear there—sky
illumines it the other horizontal side dark (night)
existing at once 'brought on' together?

L   when?   OR   appear
    a pear   this
    falling   mined
    a star   —if
    dropping   is—
    is   past
    dark—in   —or
    only day   —but I see
                            —the
    there   —if illumined
                            straightforwardness

L   accidentally.

*L and R stand amidst the floating brains-jewels though not
behind any of them:*

L   What is the left hand?—immediately MR shouting
    and running on them with a horn in the center of his
    forehead—one would muse, think—then he'd run in
    hollering, a green moss-covered sloth that's hanging at
                        once in the midst of the rhino
                as he moves through the sir yelling

Yet concentrating, I answered the question, extending
the left hand—"*This* is the
left hand," but
I didn't say it—I extended
it soundlessly.

*OR is front stage in the spot where she began (at the beginning of
the play). MR is curled as sloth with his back to the audience
hanging on the shelf-branch.*

OR   *now*
       dreamed
       I hit the sun
       last night
       with my hand

       someone in
              the dream
       was teaching
              me how
       to put my hand
       up
              properly

*After speaking she puts up one hand, just holds it up
briefly, not a salute.*

THE END

About the Author

Born in Santa Barbara, California, in 1944, Leslie Scalapino
received a Bachelor's degree from Reed College and an M.A. in
English from UC Berkeley. Her numerous collections of poetry
include: *It's go in horizontal: Selected Poems 1974-2006* (University
of California Press, 2008); *Zither & Autobiography* (2003); *The
Tango* (2001); *New Time* (1999); *Sight* (1999), a collaboration with
Lyn Hejinian; *way* (1988), which was the recipient of the Ameri-
can Book Award; *that they were at the beach* (1985); *Considering
how exaggerated music is* (1982); and *O and Other Poems* (1976).

She is also the author of many plays and works of prose, such
as *The Weatherman Turns Himself In* (1999), *Dahlia's Iris: Secret
Autobiography and Fiction* (2003), *The Public World / Syntactically
Impermanence* (1999), *Green and Black, Selected Writings* (1996),
and the trilogy *The Return of Painting, The Pearl, and Orion* (1991).

As publisher, she is the founder of O Books. She has also edited
numerous books, including *The Collected Poems of Philip Whalen*
(2007).

Scalapino has taught at the Naropa Institute, Bard College, and
UC San Diego, where her papers are currently being held in the
Mandeville Special Collections Library.

She currently lives in Oakland, California, where she teaches at
Mills College.

About Chax Press

Chax Press was founded in 1984 by Charles Alexander as a creator of handmade fine arts editions of literature, often with an inventive and playful sense of how the book arts might interact with innovative writing. Beginning in 1990 the press started to publish works in trade paperback editions, such as the book you hold. We currently occupy studio space, shared with the painter Cynthia Miller, in the Small Planet Bakery building at the north side of downtown Tucson, Arizona. Recent and forthcoming books by Alice Notley, Barbara Henning, Charles Bernstein, Anne Waldman, Tenney Nathanson, Linh Dinh, Mark Weiss, Nico Vassilakis, Robert Mittenthal, Jonathan Stalling, Will Alexander, and many more, may be found on our web site at *http://chax.org*.

Chax Press projects are supported by the Tucson Pima Arts Council, by the Arizona Commission on the Arts (with funding from the State of Arizona and the National Endowment for the Arts), by The Southwestern Foundation, and by many individual donors who keep us at work at the edges of contemporary literature through their generosity, friendship, and good spirits.

This book is set in Eric Gill's Gill Sans typeface in 10 and 11 point size with other sizes used for titling. Composition and design in Adobe InDesign.

TUCSON PIMA
ARTS
COUNCIL

Arizona
Commission
on the Arts

NATIONAL
ENDOWMENT
FOR THE ARTS